The Travell Capital System

Turn Everyday Spending into Flights, Hotels, and Premium Travel Without Paying Full Price Using Points, Miles, and Rewards

SATYAJIT PAL

This book is intended for informational and educational purposes only. It reflects the author's personal research, analysis, and experience in the field of travel rewards, points, and credit card systems. While every effort has been made to ensure accuracy, the information presented may change over time due to updates in airline programs, credit card policies, and market conditions.

The author does not guarantee specific results. Readers are encouraged to conduct their own research and make decisions based on their individual financial situation and risk tolerance.

The publisher and platform are not responsible for the content of this book or any outcomes resulting from its use.

Made with ❤ on the Notion Press Platform

www.notionpress.com

Contents

You are not poor.

You are simply using your money without a system

Introduction

Most people believe that luxury travel is only for a small group of people. They think business class flights, premium hotels, and high-end travel experiences require a very high income.

That belief feels true. It looks true. But it is not entirely accurate. The difference is not income alone. The difference is how money is used.

Every month, money moves through your life. You spend on food, subscriptions, shopping, travel, and everyday needs. For most people, that money disappears after the transaction is complete.

For a small group of people, that same spending becomes something else. It becomes travel opportunities.

This book will help you understand that difference. Most travel systems are built in a way that works against you.

Airlines and hotels change prices constantly. The same flight can cost very different amounts depending on the day, the time, and the demand. If you are paying in cash, you are always reacting to these changes.

There is another layer that most people never learn.

Behind every airline and hotel system, there is a structured network of points and rewards. These systems are more predictable than cash prices. When used correctly, they give you control.

That is where the advantage exists.

What This Book Will Do for You

This is not a collection of random tips.

This is a system.

You will learn how to:

Turn everyday spending into travel value

Multiply rewards using simple but structured methods

Convert points into real travel experiences

Avoid common mistakes that reduce value

More importantly, you will learn how to think differently about spending.

The Core Model

This book is built on a simple structure:

Spend. Earn. Convert. Redeem.

Most people stop at spending.

Some people earn points.

Very few understand how to convert and redeem in a smart way.

That gap is where most value is lost.

This book will help you close that gap.

Who This Book Is For

This book is for:

Professionals who want better travel experiences without increasing spending

Individuals who already spend money every month but gain nothing extra from it

Beginners who want a clear and structured starting point

People who have tried using points but feel they are not getting real value

You do not need advanced knowledge.

You need a clear approach.

What This Book Is Not

This is not:

- A list of popular credit cards
- A collection of shortcuts without logic
- A country specific manual

The ideas in this book are practical and can be adapted anywhere.

By the end of this book, you will not look at spending in the same way again.

CHAPTER 1

Why Travel Pricing Is Broken

Most people think travel is expensive.

They search for flights or hotels, see high prices, and assume that premium travel is not meant for them. They either delay travel or compromise on quality.

This reaction is understandable. But it is based on incomplete information.

The Illusion of Price

When you look at a flight price, you are not seeing a fixed number.

You are seeing a price that is constantly changing.

Airlines adjust prices based on:

- Demand
- Time of booking
- Season
- Seat availability

This means:

- Two people can pay very different prices for the same seat
- Prices can change within hours
- There is no fixed standard

Cash pricing is unstable.

You are always reacting to it.

Why Cash Alone Limits You

Cash is simple. It gives you direct access.

But it also has limits.

When you pay in cash:

- The transaction ends immediately
- There is no long-term value
- There is no multiplier effect

Each purchase stands alone.

There is no accumulation.

A Different Layer Exists

There is another system working in parallel.

Airlines and hotels use:

- Points
- Miles
- Reward balances

These are not just incentives. They are part of a structured system.

When you use this system properly, you can access:

- Fixed value redemption options
- Premium seats at lower effective cost
- Better travel outcomes without increasing spending

This is where the real shift happens.

The Advantage of Structured Systems

Cash transactions are straightforward.

Points based systems are structured.

With the right approach, points can:

- Accumulate over time
- Be transferred across programs
- Be used when value is highest

This creates flexibility and leverage.

Where Most People Lose Value

Many people already earn points.

But they do not use them well.

Common issues include:

- Redeeming points for low value options
- Ignoring transfer opportunities
- Using points too early without planning

The system is available.

The understanding is missing.

What This Means for You

If you rely only on cash, you stay exposed to changing prices.

If you understand how to use points, you gain control.

This is not about spending more.

It is about using what you already spend in a smarter way.

What Comes Next

Now that you understand the problem, the next step is to understand how points actually work.

In the next chapter, we will break down the structure of reward systems and how you can start using them with clarity.

CHAPTER 2

How Points Actually Work

Points look simple on the surface.

You spend money. You earn points. You use them later.

Most people stop at this level of understanding.

That is where the confusion begins.

Points Are Not Money

The first thing to understand is that points are not cash.

They behave differently.

Cash has a fixed value.

One dollar is always one dollar.

Points do not work that way.

Their value changes based on how you use them.

The same number of points can give you very different outcomes depending on where and how you redeem them.

This is why some people feel points are useless, while others extract significant value from them.

The system is the same. The approach is different.

The Three Types of Points

Not all points are created equal.

To use them effectively, you need to understand the basic categories.

Fixed Value Points

These points have a predictable value.

You redeem them directly for travel or purchases at a fixed rate.

They are simple and easy to use.

But they rarely give you exceptional value.

Transferable Points

These are the most powerful type.

They allow you to move your points into airline or hotel programs.

Once transferred, you can access better redemption options.

This is where most high value travel happens.

Program Specific Points

These points belong to a single airline or hotel program.

They cannot be moved easily.

They can still be useful, but they offer less flexibility.

Why Transferable Points Matter

Transferable points give you options.

Instead of being locked into one system, you can choose where to use them based on value.

This creates leverage.

For example, the same number of points might give you:

- A low value redemption through a fixed system
- A high value redemption through a transfer partner

The difference is not small. It can be significant.

Earning Points Is Only the Beginning

Most people focus on earning.

They look for:

- Higher reward rates
- Bonus categories

- Sign up offers

This is useful.

But earning alone does not create value.

If you earn points without a plan, you will likely redeem them in a low value way.

The real advantage comes from combining earning with a clear strategy.

Understanding Redemption Value

The value of points depends on what you get in return.

A simple way to think about it is:

- How much would this cost in cash
- How many points are required

If the points required are low compared to the cash price, the value is high.

If the points required are high compared to the cash price, the value is low.

This difference is what you are optimizing.

Why Most Redemptions Are Poor

Many people redeem points for:

- Gift cards
- Small purchases
- Low value travel

These options are easy.

They are also inefficient.

The system is designed to make these redemptions convenient, not valuable.

Convenience often comes at the cost of value.

Timing Changes Everything

Points are not just about where you redeem.

They are also about when.

Availability, promotions, and transfer bonuses all affect the outcome.

A redemption that looks average today might become excellent during a promotional window.

This is why patience and timing matter.

Building a Points Mindset

To use points effectively, you need to change how you think about spending.

Instead of asking:

What am I buying

Start asking:

What am I earning from this purchase

Over time, this shift creates a different outcome.

Spending becomes a tool instead of an expense.

What This Means for You

Points are not complicated.

But they require intention.

If you treat them casually, you will get average results.

If you treat them as part of a system, you can extract real value.

What Comes Next

Now that you understand how points work, the next step is learning how to earn them efficiently.

In the next chapter, we will focus on how to choose the right cards and structure your spending to build momentum quickly.

CHAPTER 3

Earning Points Efficiently

Earning points is where most people begin.

They sign up for a card, make a few purchases, and see points accumulate slowly. It feels like progress, but the pace is often disappointing.

After some time, many people lose interest.

The problem is not the system.

The problem is how the system is used.

Not All Spending Is Equal

Every dollar you spend does not generate the same outcome.

- Some categories earn more points.
- Some earn very little.

For example:

Travel and dining often earn higher rewards

Everyday categories may earn less

If you do not pay attention to this difference, you lose potential value every month.

The goal is not to spend more.

The goal is to direct your existing spending in a smarter way.

The Role of Credit Cards

Credit cards are the primary tool for earning points.

But they are only effective when used with intention.

Many people choose cards based on popularity or recommendations. They do not consider how those cards fit their own spending patterns.

This leads to poor results.

The right card is not the most popular one.

It is the one that aligns with how you already spend.

Welcome Bonuses Create Momentum

One of the fastest ways to build a points balance is through welcome bonuses.

These are offered when you meet a minimum spending requirement within a set time period.

For example:

- Spend a certain amount in the first three months
- Receive a large number of points as a bonus

This can accelerate your progress significantly.

However, this strategy requires discipline.

You should never increase spending just to meet a bonus requirement. The goal is to use planned expenses, not create new ones.

Category Optimization

Once you have the right card, the next step is to use it correctly.

Different cards reward different categories.

To earn efficiently, you need to:

Use the right card for the right purchase

Avoid using a single card for everything

For example:

- One card for dining
- Another for travel
- Another for online purchases

This may seem like a small adjustment.

Over time, it creates a noticeable difference.

Everyday Spending as a System

Most people treat spending as a series of isolated decisions.

They pay when needed and move on.

A more effective approach is to treat spending as a system.

Each transaction becomes part of a larger structure.

You begin to think in terms of:

- Monthly patterns
- Category allocation
- Reward outcomes

This shift turns routine spending into a steady source of value.

Avoiding Common Mistakes

Many people lose value because of simple errors.

Common mistakes include:

- Using debit instead of credit for reward categories
- Ignoring bonus categories
- Spreading spending across too many cards without a plan
- Missing bonus deadlines

These mistakes are easy to avoid once you are aware of them.

The Balance Between Simplicity and Efficiency

It is easy to overcomplicate this process.

Using too many cards or tracking too many categories can become difficult.

The goal is to find a balance.

You want enough structure to capture value, but not so much complexity that it becomes hard to maintain.

A simple system used consistently is more effective than a complex system used occasionally.

Tracking Your Progress

If you do not track your points, it becomes difficult to improve.

You do not need a complicated tool.

A simple method is enough.

Track:

- Total points earned each month
- Spending by category
- Progress toward specific goals

This gives you clarity.

Clarity leads to better decisions.

Building Momentum Over Time

Earning points is not about immediate results.

It is about consistency.

Small improvements in how you spend can compound over time.

What feels like a minor adjustment today can create significant value over several months.

This is how momentum builds.

What This Means for You

You already spend money every month.

That is not the problem.

The opportunity lies in how that spending is directed.

When you align your spending with the right structure, earning points becomes predictable.

Predictability creates control.

What Comes Next

Now that you understand how to earn points efficiently, the next step is to multiply them.

In the next chapter, we will look at how to stack rewards, use transfer partners, and unlock higher value from the same points.

CHAPTER 4

Stacking and Multipliers

Most people stop after earning points.

They use a card, collect rewards, and wait for the balance to grow. This approach works, but it is slow.

There is another layer that changes the outcome.

This is where stacking and multipliers come in.

What Stacking Really Means

Stacking is the process of earning rewards from a single transaction in more than one way.

Instead of receiving one benefit, you combine multiple systems to increase the total outcome.

For example, a single purchase can generate:

- Base reward points from your card
- Bonus points from a category offer
- Additional rewards from a shopping platform

Each layer adds to the final result.

Individually, these gains may seem small. Together, they create a meaningful difference.

Why Most People Do Not Stack

The idea is simple, but the execution is often ignored.

Common reasons include:

- Lack of awareness
- Perceived complexity
- Habit of using the same method for every purchase

Once you understand the structure, stacking becomes easier to apply.

It does not require constant effort. It requires a consistent approach.

The Power of Multipliers

Multipliers increase the number of points you earn for each unit of spending.

Instead of earning one point per dollar, you may earn two, three, or more depending on the category or promotion.

This changes the pace of accumulation.

For example:

- A standard transaction earns at a base rate
- A bonus category increases that rate
- A promotional offer increases it further

The same spending produces a different outcome.

Combining Stacking and Multipliers

Stacking and multipliers work best when used together.

A well-structured transaction can include:

- A card that offers a high earning rate
- A category that provides additional rewards
- A platform that adds another layer of benefit

This creates a compound effect.

The goal is not to chase every possible offer.

The goal is to recognize opportunities where these elements align naturally.

Practical Example

Consider a simple scenario.

You make a purchase for a planned expense.

Instead of completing the transaction directly, you:

- Use a card that offers a higher reward rate for that category
- Complete the purchase through a platform that provides additional rewards
- Take advantage of a temporary promotion

The result is a higher number of points from the same spending.

Nothing extra was purchased. The approach changed.

Promotions and Limited Time Opportunities

Promotions are an important part of this system.

They can include:

- Temporary bonus categories
- Increased transfer rates
- Special offers from partners

These opportunities do not last long.

They require attention and timing.

You do not need to follow every promotion.

You need to recognize the ones that align with your goals.

Avoiding Overcomplication

It is easy to turn stacking into a complicated process.

Using too many tools or chasing every offer can create confusion.

The goal is not perfection.

The goal is improvement.

A simple structure that you can follow consistently is more valuable than a complex system that you abandon.

Building Your Personal System

To use stacking effectively, you need a repeatable approach.

Start with:

- A small number of cards that match your spending
- A clear understanding of your main categories
- Awareness of a few reliable platforms or partners

From there, you can gradually improve.

You do not need to apply every technique at once.

Consistency matters more than variety.

The Role of Awareness

Stacking opportunities are often hidden in plain sight.

They exist within:

- Payment methods
- Platform choices
- Timing of purchases

Once you start looking for them, you will notice patterns.

This awareness is what turns a basic system into an efficient one.

What This Means for You

You are already spending money.

That part does not change.

What changes is how much value you extract from each transaction.

Stacking and multipliers allow you to increase that value without increasing your spending.

What Comes Next

Now that you understand how to increase your earning potential, the next step is to use your points wisely.

In the next chapter, we will focus on redemption strategies and how to turn your points into high value travel experiences.

CHAPTER 5

Redeeming Like a Pro

Earning points feels satisfying.

You see the balance grow. You feel progress. It gives a sense of movement.

But points have no real value until they are used.

This is where most people lose the advantage.

Redemption Is Where Value Is Created

Points are not valuable by themselves.

They become valuable only when they are exchanged for something meaningful.

The difference between a good system and an average one is not how many points you earn.

It is how you use them.

Two people can earn the same number of points and get very different outcomes.

- One may use them for small purchases.
- The other may use them for premium travel.

The gap in value can be significant.

Understanding Value in Simple Terms

When you redeem points, you are making a choice.

You are deciding what those points are worth to you.

A simple way to think about it is:

- What is the cash price of this option
- How many points are required

If the points required are low compared to the cash price, the value is high.

If the points required are high compared to the cash price, the value is low.

This is the basic lens you should apply every time.

Why Premium Travel Gives Better Value

In most cases, the best use of points is for premium travel.

This includes:

- Business class flights
- First class flights
- High end hotel stays

The reason is simple.

Cash prices for these options are usually high.

Points requirements do not always increase at the same rate.

This creates an opportunity.

You can access experiences that would normally be expensive, using a smaller effective cost.

The Trap of Easy Redemptions

Many programs offer simple ways to use points.

These include:

- Gift cards
- Small purchases
- Direct statement credits

These options are easy to use.

They are also low in value.

They are designed for convenience, not efficiency.

If you choose convenience every time, you lose the advantage of the system.

Timing Matters in Redemption

When you redeem points is just as important as how you redeem them.

Availability changes.

Promotions appear and disappear.

Transfer bonuses can increase your value for a limited time.

If you rush into redemption without checking these factors, you may miss better opportunities.

Patience can improve outcomes.

Planning Before You Redeem

Before using your points, take a moment to plan.

Ask yourself:

- What is my goal
- What options are available
- Which option gives the best value

Even a simple plan can prevent poor decisions.

Redemption should not be an afterthought.

It should be intentional.

Avoiding Common Redemption Mistakes

There are a few patterns that reduce value consistently.

These include:

- Using points as soon as they are available without a goal
- Choosing low value options for convenience
- Ignoring transfer opportunities
- Not comparing cash and points options

These mistakes are easy to avoid once you are aware of them.

Flexibility Creates Better Outcomes

If you are flexible with:

- Travel dates
- Routes
- Destinations

You increase your chances of finding better redemption options.

Rigid plans limit your choices.

A small adjustment in timing or route can lead to a much better outcome.

The Role of Awareness

Good redemption decisions come from awareness.

You need to:

- Understand how different programs work
- Recognize good opportunities
- Avoid low value options

This does not require constant effort.

It requires a basic level of attention.

What This Means for You

You have already learned how to earn and multiply points.

Now you understand how to use them.

This is where the system becomes complete.

Without proper redemption, earning has limited impact.

With proper redemption, the same points can unlock significantly more value.

What Comes Next

Now that you know how to redeem points effectively, the next step is to design your overall travel strategy.

In the next chapter, we will focus on how to set clear goals and align your points with real travel outcomes.

CHAPTER 6

Transfer Partners Explained

At this stage, you understand how to earn points and how to redeem them.

But there is one layer that changes everything.

This is the concept of transfer partners.

It is often the difference between average results and high value outcomes.

What Transfer Partners Are

Transfer partners allow you to move your points from one system into another.

Most commonly, this means:

- Moving points from a credit card program
- Into an airline or hotel loyalty program

Once transferred, your points follow the rules of the new program.

This opens up more options.

Why Transfers Matter

Without transfers, your points remain limited.

You can only use them within a fixed system.

With transfers, you gain access to:

- More airlines
- More hotel programs
- Better redemption options

This increases flexibility.

Flexibility creates better outcomes.

A Simple Way to Understand Transfers

Think of your points as a currency.

In one system, they have a certain value.

When you transfer them to another system, that value can change.

In some cases, the value increases.

In other cases, it may not.

The goal is to move your points only when it improves your outcome.

The Role of Conversion Ratios

Not all transfers are equal.

Each transfer partner has a conversion ratio.

For example:

- A 1:1 ratio means one point becomes one point

- A different ratio may reduce or increase the value

Understanding this is important.

A transfer may look attractive, but if the ratio is not favourable, the value can decrease.

Always check before transferring.

When Transfers Create Value

Transfers are most useful when:

- You find a high value redemption in a partner program
- The conversion ratio is reasonable
- The final outcome is better than using points directly

This usually happens with:

- Premium flights
- Long distance travel
- Specific airline partnerships

These situations create opportunities.

Transfer Bonuses

Sometimes, programs offer temporary bonuses.

For example:

Transfer points and receive extra value for a limited time.

This can improve your outcome significantly.

However, bonuses should not be the only reason to transfer.

Always start with the final goal.

Then decide if the bonus supports it.

The Risk of Transferring Too Early

Once points are transferred, they usually cannot be moved back.

This is important.

If you transfer points without a clear plan, you may:

- Lock them into a program you do not use
- Miss better opportunities elsewhere

The safest approach is simple.

Transfer only when:

- You are ready to redeem
- You have confirmed availability

Availability Matters

Before transferring, check if the option you want is actually available.

For example:

- A flight seat
- A hotel room

If you transfer first and check later, you may not find what you need.

This creates frustration and reduces flexibility.

Always reverse the process.

Check first. Transfer later.

Building a Transfer Strategy

You do not need to know every transfer partner.

Start with a few.

Focus on:

- Programs that match your travel goals
- Partners that offer consistent value
- Systems that are easy to use

Over time, you can expand your knowledge.

A simple approach is enough in the beginning.

Common Mistakes to Avoid

There are a few patterns that reduce value:

- Transferring points without a clear redemption plan
- Ignoring conversion ratios

- Chasing transfer bonuses without purpose
- Locking points into a single program too early

These mistakes are avoidable.

Awareness is enough.

What This Means for You

Transfer partners give you control.

Instead of being limited to one system, you can choose where your points create the most value.

This is a shift.

You move from passive usage to active decision making.

That is where the real advantage lies.

What Comes Next

Now that you understand transfer partners, the next step is to refine your redemption strategy further.

In the next chapter, we will focus on how to choose between flights and hotels and where points create the most impact.

CHAPTER 7

Flights vs Hotels Strategy

At some point, you will face a simple decision.

Should you use your points for flights or for hotels?

On the surface, this looks like a preference.

In reality, it is a strategic choice.

The way you answer this question will affect how much value you extract from your points.

Not All Redemptions Are Equal

Flights and hotels operate under different systems.

- They follow different pricing patterns.
- They offer different types of value.

If you treat them the same, you may lose opportunities.

The goal is not to choose one over the other blindly.

The goal is to understand where each one works best.

Why Flights Often Provide Higher Value

Flights, especially premium flights, tend to offer higher redemption value.

This is because:

- Cash prices for premium cabins are high
- Points requirements do not always rise at the same pace

This creates a gap.

You can use points to access experiences that would otherwise be expensive.

Business class and long-distance flights are common examples.

In many cases, this is where points deliver their strongest impact.

When Hotels Make Sense

Hotels are different.

They provide value in a more consistent way.

You can use points for:

- Short stays
- Extended trips
- Flexible travel plans

Hotels can be useful when:

- You want to reduce overall trip cost
- You are planning multiple nights
- You value convenience over optimization

They may not always give the highest value per point, but they can still play an important role.

The Role of Trip Type

Your decision should depend on the type of trip.

For example:

- A long international trip may benefit more from flight redemptions
- A short domestic trip may benefit more from hotel savings

There is no single rule.

Context matters.

Splitting Your Strategy

You do not need to choose only one.

A balanced approach often works best.

For example:

Use points for flights where value is high

Use cash or lower value points for hotels

Or:

Use points for hotels when flight prices are already reasonable

This flexibility helps you adapt.

Comparing Value Before Deciding

Before making a decision, compare both options.

Ask:

- What is the cash cost of the flight
- What is the cash cost of the hotel
- How many points are required for each

This comparison gives you clarity.

It helps you see where your points will create the most impact.

Avoiding Emotional Decisions

Travel decisions are often emotional.

You may feel tempted to use points quickly just to reduce a visible cost.

For example:

Using points for a hotel because it feels like saving money

But this may not be the best use of your points.

A better approach is to pause and evaluate.

Focus on overall value, not immediate savings.

Flexibility Improves Outcomes

If you remain flexible, you increase your options.

Flexibility in:

- Travel dates
- Destinations
- Accommodation choices

This allows you to choose the better option between flights and hotels.

Rigid plans reduce your ability to optimize.

Building a Personal Preference

Over time, you will develop your own pattern.

Some people prefer:

- Using points for premium flights

Others prefer:

- Reducing total trip cost through hotels

Both approaches can work.

The key is to be intentional.

What This Means for You

Points give you options.

Flights and hotels are two different ways to use them.

When you understand how each works, you can decide with clarity.

You are no longer reacting.

You are choosing.

What Comes Next

Now that you understand where to use your points, the next step is to go deeper into premium travel.

In the next chapter, we will focus on how to book business class flights at a lower effective cost.

CHAPTER 8

Flights vs Hotels Strategy

At some point, you will face a simple decision.

Should you use your points for flights or for hotels?

On the surface, this looks like a preference.

In reality, it is a strategic choice.

The way you answer this question will affect how much value you extract from your points.

Why Business Class Feels Expensive

When you search for a premium seat, you usually see a high cash price.

This price reflects:

- Comfort
- Space
- Service
- Demand

For many travelers, this becomes the final answer.

They either choose a lower class or avoid the trip.

But cash pricing is only one side of the system.

Points Change the Equation

When you use points, the structure changes.

The price you see in cash is not always aligned with the points required.

In many cases:

- Cash prices rise sharply for premium cabins
- Points requirements increase at a slower rate

This creates an opportunity.

You can access business class using fewer resources than expected.

Understanding Award Availability

Not every seat is available for points.

Airlines release a limited number of seats for redemption.

These seats depend on:

- Route
- Timing
- Demand

If you search randomly, you may not find availability.

This leads many people to believe that business class redemption is not possible.

In reality, it requires a more structured approach.

Planning Ahead

Availability improves when you plan in advance.

Airlines often release seats:

- Several months before departure
- At specific intervals

If you wait until the last moment, your options become limited.

Planning early gives you more control.

Being Flexible

Flexibility is one of the most important factors.

If you are open to:

- Adjusting travel dates
- Considering nearby airports
- Exploring alternate routes

You increase your chances of finding a good redemption.

Small adjustments can make a large difference.

Choosing the Right Routes

Not all routes offer the same opportunities.

Some routes:

- Have more frequent flights
- Offer better redemption options
- Provide consistent availability

Others may be limited or highly competitive.

Understanding this helps you focus your efforts.

Using Transfer Partners Effectively

Transfer partners play a key role in booking business class.

Instead of using points directly, you can:

- Move points into an airline program
- Use that program to access better options

This often leads to:

- Lower points requirements
- Better seat availability
- Access to partner airlines

This is where strategy becomes important.

Avoiding Common Mistakes

Many people miss good opportunities because of simple errors.

These include:

- Searching without a plan
- Ignoring alternate routes
- Transferring points before checking availability
- Booking the first option without comparison

These mistakes reduce your chances of success.

Awareness helps you avoid them.

Understanding the Trade-Off

Booking business class with points may require effort.

You may need to:

- Search multiple options
- Wait for availability
- Adjust your plans

This effort replaces the need to spend a large amount of cash.

It is a trade-off.

For many people, the outcome is worth it.

The Experience Difference

Business class is not only about comfort.

It changes the entire travel experience.

You get:

- Better seating
- More space
- Improved service
- A more relaxed journey

When you use points effectively, you can access this experience without paying the full cash price.

What This Means for You

Business class is not limited to a small group of travelers.

It becomes accessible when you understand how the system works.

Points, when used correctly, allow you to shift from basic travel to premium experiences.

This is one of the most powerful outcomes of the system.

CHAPTER 9

Avoiding Bad Redemptions

Earning points takes effort.

You plan your spending, choose the right cards, and build your balance over time. This process creates value.

But that value can be lost quickly.

It often happens in a single decision.

What a Bad Redemption Looks Like

A bad redemption is not always obvious.

It usually feels convenient. It may even feel like a smart choice in the moment.

In reality, it provides very little value compared to what your points could achieve.

Examples include:

- Using points for small purchases
- Redeeming for low value options because they are easy
- Ignoring better alternatives

The problem is not the action itself.

The problem is the lost opportunity.

The Cost of Convenience

Convenience is one of the biggest reasons people make poor decisions.

Programs are designed to make certain redemptions simple:

- Gift cards
- Direct discounts
- Small purchases

These options are easy to use.

They require no planning.

But they also deliver low value.

When you choose convenience repeatedly, you reduce the overall impact of your points.

Not All Savings Are Equal

Saving money feels good.

But not all savings are meaningful.

For example:

- Saving a small amount on a purchase using points
- Compared to saving a large amount on a premium flight

Both are technically savings.

Only one creates significant value.

The difference lies in how points are used.

Redeeming Without a Goal

Many people redeem points as soon as they have enough.

There is no plan.

There is no clear outcome.

This leads to scattered usage.

Points are used here and there without creating a meaningful result.

A better approach is to define a goal first.

Then align your redemptions with that goal.

Ignoring Better Options

Sometimes better options exist, but they are not explored.

This can happen when:

- You do not compare different programs
- You do not check transfer possibilities
- You accept the first available option

A few extra minutes of checking can reveal better outcomes.

Awareness makes a difference.

Transferring Without Purpose

Transfers are powerful, but they can also create problems.

If you transfer points without a clear plan, you may:

- Lock your points into a single program
- Lose flexibility
- Miss better opportunities elsewhere

Once transferred, points are difficult to move again.

This makes planning essential.

Overvaluing Simplicity

Simple options often feel safe.

They require less effort.

But simplicity does not always mean efficiency.

A slightly more complex process can produce a much better result.

The goal is not to avoid effort completely.

The goal is to apply effort where it creates value.

The Role of Patience

Good redemptions do not always appear immediately.

They may require:

- Waiting for availability
- Monitoring options
- Adjusting plans

Impatience leads to quick decisions.

Quick decisions often lead to lower value.

Patience improves outcomes.

Learning From Each Redemption

Every redemption is a learning opportunity.

After using your points, ask:

- Was this the best option available
- Could the value have been higher
- What would I do differently next time

This reflection helps you improve over time.

Building a Decision Framework

To avoid poor redemptions, you need a simple framework.

Before using your points, consider:

- What is the goal
- What are the available options
- Which option provides the highest value

This does not require complex analysis.

It requires a consistent habit.

What This Means for You

Your points represent accumulated effort.

Every redemption decision determines how much of that effort is realized.

Good decisions increase value.

Poor decisions reduce it.

When you approach redemption with awareness and intention, you protect your progress.

What Comes Next

Now that you understand how to avoid losing value, the next step is to design your overall travel strategy.

In the next chapter, we will focus on setting clear goals and aligning your points with real travel outcomes.

CHAPTER 10

Designing Your Travel Goal

Up to this point, you have learned how to earn, multiply, and use points.

Now comes the step that connects everything.

You need a clear travel goal.

Without a goal, your efforts remain scattered.

With a goal, your system becomes focused.

Why a Clear Goal Matters

Many people collect points without direction.

They earn steadily but do not know what they are working toward.

This leads to:

- Random redemptions
- Low value usage
- Lack of motivation

A clear goal changes this.

It gives your points a purpose.

Moving From Idea to Structure

A goal is not just a destination.

It needs to be defined clearly.

Instead of thinking:

"I want to travel"

Think:

- Where do I want to go
- When do I want to go
- What kind of experience do I want

Clarity turns an idea into a plan.

Defining the Experience

Travel goals are not only about location.

They are also about experience.

For example:

- Economy travel or business class
- Budget stay or premium hotel
- Short trip or extended stay

These choices affect how many points you need.

They also shape your strategy.

Estimating the Requirement

Once your goal is defined, you need to estimate what it will take.

This includes:

- Points required for flights
- Points required for hotels
- Additional costs if any

You do not need perfect accuracy.

A rough estimate is enough to begin.

This gives you a target.

Understanding the Timeline

Every goal has a timeline.

Some trips can be planned within a few months.

Others may take longer.

Your timeline depends on:

- Your earning rate
- Your spending patterns
- Your strategy

Understanding this helps you stay realistic.

Aligning Points with the Goal

Once you know your requirement and timeline, you can align your actions.

This includes:

- Choosing the right cards
- Using the right categories
- Timing your spending

Each step becomes connected to your goal.

This creates direction.

Avoiding Unrealistic Expectations

It is easy to set ambitious goals.

But unrealistic goals can lead to frustration.

If the gap between your current position and your target is too large, progress may feel slow.

A better approach is to:

- Start with a realistic goal
- Build confidence
- Expand gradually

This keeps you engaged.

Adjusting as You Progress

Your plan does not need to remain fixed.

As you learn more and your points grow, you can adjust:

- Your destination
- Your timeline
- Your experience level

Flexibility allows you to improve your outcome.

Breaking the Goal into Steps

Large goals can feel distant.

Breaking them into smaller steps helps.

For example:

- First milestone: reach a certain number of points
- Second milestone: identify possible options
- Third milestone: confirm availability

Each step moves you forward.

Progress becomes visible.

Staying Consistent

A clear goal makes consistency easier.

When you know what you are working toward, small actions feel meaningful.

Over time, these actions build momentum.

Consistency is more important than intensity.

What This Means for You

Your points are not just a balance.

They are a path to a specific outcome.

When you define your goal clearly, your system becomes focused.

You stop reacting and start planning.

This is where real progress begins.

What Comes Next

Now that you have a defined goal, the next step is to understand how fast you can reach it.

In the next chapter, we will focus on points velocity and how to measure your progress over time.

CHAPTER 11

Points Velocity and Timeline

You now have a clear goal.

You understand how to earn, multiply, and use points.

The next question is simple.

- How long will it take to reach your goal

This is where points velocity comes in.

What Points Velocity Means

Points velocity is the rate at which you earn points over time.

It answers a practical question.

- How fast is your balance growing

Without this understanding, your goal remains abstract.

With it, your goal becomes measurable.

Why Velocity Matters?

Many people collect points without tracking their progress.

They know they are earning, but they do not know how fast.

This creates uncertainty.

You may feel like you are moving forward, but you cannot tell if you are on track.

Velocity removes that uncertainty.

It gives you clarity.

Calculating Your Earning Rate

You do not need a complex system.

Start with a simple estimate.

Track:

- Total points earned in a month
- Average spending across categories
- Bonus points from promotions or offers

From this, you can calculate a monthly earning rate.

This becomes your baseline.

Connecting Velocity to Your Goal

Once you know your earning rate, you can compare it to your target.

For example:

- Total points required for your goal
- Points earned per month

This allows you to estimate your timeline.

You move from guessing to planning.

Understanding the Timeline

Your timeline depends on:

- Your monthly earning rate
- Your use of multipliers and bonuses
- Your ability to optimize spending

A higher velocity shortens your timeline.

A lower velocity extends it.

This relationship is simple, but powerful.

Increasing Your Velocity

If your timeline feels too long, you have options.

You can increase your velocity by:

- Using higher earning categories
- Taking advantage of welcome bonuses
- Applying stacking strategies
- Timing your spending with promotions

Each improvement adds to your monthly total.

Over time, this creates a noticeable difference.

Avoiding Unrealistic Expectations

It is important to stay realistic.

Not every goal can be achieved quickly.

If your target requires a large number of points, it may take time.

Trying to accelerate too aggressively can lead to poor decisions.

A steady approach is more effective.

Tracking Progress Over Time

Tracking does not need to be complicated.

A simple monthly review is enough.

Check:

- Points earned
- Progress toward your goal
- Any changes in your strategy

This keeps you aligned.

It also helps you adjust when needed.

The Role of Consistency

Velocity is not about one large jump.

It is about consistent progress.

Small improvements applied regularly create momentum.

Momentum builds over time.

This is how goals become achievable.

Adjusting Your Plan

Your initial plan is not fixed.

As your situation changes, your velocity may change as well.

You may:

- Increase your earning rate
- Discover better strategies
- Refine your approach

These adjustments help you stay on track.

What This Means for You

Points are not just a balance.

They represent movement toward a goal.

Velocity tells you how fast you are moving.

When you understand your pace, you gain control.

You can plan, adjust, and improve with confidence.

What Comes Next

Now that you understand your timeline, the next step is to bring everything together into action.

In the next chapter, we will focus on a clear execution plan that helps you move from understanding to results.

CHAPTER 12

Execution Plan

You now understand the system.

You know how to earn points, multiply them, convert them, and redeem them with purpose.

You have a defined goal.

You understand your timeline.

The only step left is execution.

Why Execution Matters

Understanding creates potential.

Execution creates results.

Many people stop after learning. They gather information, explore options, and feel prepared.

But without action, nothing changes.

This chapter is about turning your understanding into a working system.

Start With What You Already Have

You do not need to wait for the perfect setup.

Begin with:

- Your current spending
- Your existing cards
- Your immediate goals

The system does not require a complete reset.

It improves what is already in place.

Step 1: Define Your Goal Clearly

Start with a simple question.

What do you want to achieve

Be specific:

- Destination
- Travel type
- Timeline

Clarity at this stage makes every next step easier.

Step 2: Estimate Your Requirement

Based on your goal, estimate:

- Points needed for flights
- Points needed for hotels

You do not need exact numbers.

A reasonable estimate is enough to begin.

This becomes your target.

Step 3: Evaluate Your Current Position

Look at where you stand today.

Check:

- Current points balance
- Monthly spending
- Categories where you spend the most

This gives you a starting point.

Step 4: Choose Your Core Cards

Select a small number of cards that align with your spending.

Focus on:

- Cards that reward your main categories
- Programs that offer flexibility
- Systems that support your goal

Avoid using too many cards without a clear plan.

Step 5: Structure Your Spending

Now align your spending with your strategy.

For each category:

- Assign the most suitable card
- Use it consistently

This creates a predictable earning pattern.

Step 6: Apply Stacking Where Possible

Identify simple opportunities to improve your returns.

Look for:

- Bonus categories
- Platform based rewards
- Occasional promotions

Do not try to apply every technique.

Focus on a few that fit naturally into your routine.

Step 7: Monitor Your Progress

Track your points regularly.

A simple monthly review is enough.

Check:

- Points earned
- Progress toward your goal
- Any gaps in your strategy

This keeps you aligned.

Step 8: Plan Your Redemption

Before using your points, confirm:

- Availability
- Value
- Best option among alternatives

Avoid rushed decisions.

Take a few moments to compare.

Step 9: Execute With Confidence

Once everything is aligned:

- Transfer points if needed
- Complete your booking
- Confirm your outcome

Execution should feel straightforward at this stage.

Step 10: Review and Improve

After completing a redemption, reflect.

Ask:

- Did this match my goal
- Could the value have been higher
- What can I improve next time

This creates a feedback loop.

Each cycle improves your system.

Keeping the System Simple

It is easy to overcomplicate execution.

You do not need:

- Multiple complex tools
- Constant monitoring
- Perfect optimization

You need:

- A clear goal
- A consistent approach
- Basic awareness

Simplicity ensures sustainability.

What This Means for You

You now have a complete system.

From earning to redemption, each step is connected.

Execution is what turns this system into results.

Once you apply it, your approach to spending and travel changes.

What Comes Next

The next step is to see how this system works in real situations.

In the next chapter, we will look at practical examples and case studies that bring everything together.

CHAPTER 13

Real Case Studies

Understanding a system is one step.

Seeing it work in real situations is another.

Case studies help bridge this gap.

They show how the same principles can be applied in different ways, depending on the person, the goal, and the timeline.

Why Case Studies Matter

Theory gives you direction.

Examples give you confidence.

When you see how others have applied the system, it becomes easier to relate it to your own situation.

You begin to see:

- What is possible
- What is practical
- What adjustments may be needed

Case Study 1: The Focused Beginner

Profile

- Monthly spending: moderate
- No prior experience with points
- Goal: international trip within one year

Approach

This person started with a clear goal.

They selected a small number of cards that aligned with their main spending categories.

They focused on:

- Meeting welcome bonus requirements using planned expenses
- Using the correct card for each category
- Avoiding unnecessary purchases

They also tracked their points monthly.

Outcome

Within the planned timeline, they accumulated enough points for a flight redemption.

The result was not instant, but it was predictable.

The key factor was consistency.

Case Study 2: The Optimizer

Profile

- Monthly spending: higher than average
- Some experience with rewards
- Goal: premium travel experience

Approach

This person already understood basic earning.

They improved their system by:

- Applying stacking strategies
- Using transfer partners effectively
- Monitoring promotions and bonus opportunities

They were selective.

They did not chase every offer. They focused on opportunities that aligned with their goal.

Outcome

They achieved a higher value redemption using fewer points than expected.

The difference came from optimization, not additional spending.

Case Study 3: The Balanced User

Profile

- Monthly spending: consistent
- Preference for simple systems
- Goal: reduce overall travel cost

Approach

This person avoided complexity.

They:

- Used a limited number of cards
- Focused on a few key categories
- Used points for both flights and hotels based on value

They did not aim for perfect optimization.

They aimed for steady improvement.

Outcome

They reduced their travel expenses over time.

The system remained easy to maintain.

Simplicity made it sustainable.

Case Study 4: The Flexible Planner

Profile

- Monthly spending: moderate
- Flexible with travel plans
- Goal: maximize value from points

Approach

This person used flexibility as an advantage.

They:

- Adjusted travel dates based on availability
- Considered alternate routes
- Waited for better redemption opportunities

They combined this with:

- Transfer strategies
- Timing based decisions

Outcome

They achieved high value redemptions without increasing their spending.

Flexibility created better options.

Key Observations

Across all cases, a few patterns appear.

- Clear goals improve outcomes
- Consistent spending creates steady progress
- Simple systems are easier to maintain
- Awareness leads to better decisions

No single approach fits everyone.

The system adapts to the individual.

Applying These Lessons

You do not need to copy any one case.

Instead, take elements that match your situation.

Consider:

- Your spending level
- Your preferred level of effort
- Your travel goals

Then build your approach around these factors.

What This Means for You

The system works.

But it works differently for each person.

Your results will depend on how you apply the principles.

When you combine clarity, consistency, and awareness, you create a structure that delivers results over time.

Closing Thought

At the beginning, this may feel unfamiliar.

With practice, it becomes natural.

What once required effort becomes routine.

That is when the system starts working for you without constant attention.

What Comes Next

You now have the complete framework.

The final step is to bring everything together and take action.

FINAL CHAPTER

Bringing It All Together

You started this journey with a simple idea.

Travel feels expensive.

That belief is common. It is also incomplete.

What you have seen in this book is not a shortcut. It is a system.

A way to approach spending, rewards, and travel with clarity.

What Has Changed

At the beginning, spending may have felt routine.

Now it has structure.

You understand:

- How points are earned
- How they can be multiplied
- How to convert them into better options
- How to redeem them with purpose

More importantly, you understand how these steps connect.

This connection is what creates value.

From Reaction to Control

Most people react to prices.

They search, compare, and accept what is available.

This approach keeps them dependent on the system.

You now have a different approach.

You can:

- Plan before you spend
- Build points with intention
- Choose when and how to redeem

This shifts you from reacting to deciding.

The Power of Consistency

There is no single action that creates results.

It is the accumulation of small decisions.

Each time you:

- Use the right card
- Apply a simple strategy
- Avoid a poor redemption

You improve your outcome.

Over time, these small improvements build momentum.

Keeping It Practical

You do not need to apply everything at once.

Start simple.

Focus on:

- One clear goal
- A few cards that match your spending
- A consistent approach to earning and using points

As you become comfortable, you can expand.

Simplicity is what makes the system sustainable.

Your First Step

If you take nothing else from this book, take this.

Do not wait for the perfect moment.

Start with what you already have.

- Your current spending
- Your current cards
- Your immediate goals

Apply one change.

Then build from there.

A Different Way to Think About Travel

Travel does not have to be limited by price.

It can be shaped by strategy.

When you understand how the system works, you begin to see options where others see limits.

This does not mean every trip will be perfect.

It means you are no longer dependent on chance.

Where This Leads

Over time, this approach creates more than savings.

It creates:

- Better experiences
- More flexibility
- Greater control over how you travel

You move from occasional opportunities to consistent outcomes.

A Simple Reminder

Points are not the goal.

They are a tool.

The goal is the experience.

Keep this in mind as you continue.

Your Next Step

If you want to go further, the next step is to apply this system to your own situation.

Every person's spending pattern is different.

Every goal is different.

A personalized approach can make the process faster and more effective.

Continue the Journey

If you want to build a structured plan based on your spending and goals, you can explore a guided approach.

Visit:

rewardtactix.com

There, you can:

- Map your travel goal
- Understand your timeline
- Build a strategy that fits your situation

Final Thought

You now have the knowledge.

What matters next is what you do with it.

Start small. Stay consistent. Improve over time.

That is how the system works.

BONUS CHAPTER

Tools and Templates

A practical set of simple tools to help you apply the system consistently.

How to Use These Templates

This section is designed to make execution easier.

You do not need to use every template at once.

Start with:

- One clear goal
- One tracker
- One simple routine

As you become comfortable, you can expand.

Consistency matters more than complexity.

Monthly Points Tracker

Use this to track how your points grow over time.

MonthOpening | BalancePoints | EarnedPoints | UsedClosing | Balance

Notes:

- Track once per month
- Focus on overall movement, not daily changes

Category Spending Tracker

Track where your money goes.

Category	Monthly	SpendCard	UsedPoints	Earned
Dining				
Travel				
Online				
Others				
Purpose				

This helps you:

- Identify high value categories
- Adjust your card usage

Card Allocation Plan

Assign each category to a specific card.

Category	Assigned	Card	Reason
Dining			
Travel			
Online			
Bills			
Tip			

Keep it simple.

- Avoid using too many cards.

Travel Goal Planner

Define your goal clearly.

- Destination:
- Travel Type (Economy / Business Class):
- Duration:
- Target Date:
- Estimated Requirement
- Points Needed for Flights:
- Points Needed for Hotels:

Timeline Planner

Estimate how long your goal will take.

- Monthly Points Earning Rate:
- Total Points Required:
- Estimated Timeline:
- (Points Required ÷ Monthly Earning Rate)

Notes:

Adjust your strategy if the timeline feels too long.

Transaction Checklist

Before making a purchase, check:

- Am I using the right card
- Is this a bonus category
- Is there an additional reward platform
- Is there an ongoing promotion

Purpose:

This ensures you do not miss easy opportunities.

Before You Redeem Points

□ What is my goal

□ What is the cash price

□ How many points are required

□ Are better options available

□ Have I checked transfer possibilities

Reminder:

Do not rush redemption decisions.

Transfer Decision Template

Program:

- Points Available:
- Transfer Ratio:
- Redemption Option:
- Points Required:

Final Check

□ Availability confirmed

□ Transfer improves value

Common Mistakes to Avoid

□ Using points for low value options

□ Redeeming without a goal

□ Ignoring transfer opportunities

□ Missing bonus categories

□ Overcomplicating the system

Tip

Review this list once a month.

Monthly Review

Month:

- Points Earned:
- Points Used:
- Progress Toward Goal:

Reflection

- What worked well:
- What can be improved:

About The Author

Satyajit Pal is a technology professional with over 18 years of experience in IT infrastructure, identity systems, and structured problem solving. His work has consistently focused on simplifying complex systems and turning them into practical, repeatable frameworks.

Through his experience, he observed a recurring pattern. Most people spend money every month yet extract no additional value from it. The gap is not income. The gap is structure.

This insight led to the creation of this book.

Instead of treating travel as an expense, Satyajit approaches it as a system. A system where spending, rewards, and timing can be aligned to create better outcomes without increasing cost. The ideas in this book are built on that principle.

He is the creator of Rewardtactix, a platform designed to help individuals plan travel using structured reward systems, timelines, and optimized strategies. The goal is simple. Move from random spending to intentional outcomes.

To explore a personalized travel strategy based on your spending and goals, visit:

https://rewardtactix.com

Take It Further

You now understand how the system works.

The next step is to apply it to your own situation.

Every person has a different spending pattern, different goals, and a different timeline.

A structured approach can help you move faster and make better decisions.

Turn your monthly spending into a clear travel plan.

Visit:

rewardtactix.com

There, you can:

- Plan your travel goal
- Understand your timeline
- Build a strategy based on your spending

Start with clarity.
Build with consistency.

Improve over time.

Also, By The Author

If you found this book useful, explore the rest of the system:

Your First Free Flight
A Beginner's Guide to Travel Hacking with Credit Card Points and Rewards (India Edition)

Fly Business Class for Less
How to Use Points, Miles, and Hidden Airline Pricing to Travel Premium

Why You're Wasting Your Points
The Biggest Mistakes That Cost You Free Travel

From 18 Months to 6
How to Accelerate Your Points and Reach Your Travel Goals Faster

The Travel Card Stack
Build a Simple System That Earns Flights and Hotel Stays Every Month

How They Travelled for Less
Real Travel Hacking Case Studies Using Points, Miles, and Smart Spending

www.ingramcontent.com/pod-product-compliance
Lightning Source LLC
LaVergne TN
LVHW100324210926
848480LV00003B/1244
* 9 7 9 8 9 0 4 5 1 5 7 2 0 *